Father's Day 2020

Peter MAX —

　　May the LORD GOD continue to fill your heart and mind with HIS abiding presence and peace that passes all understanding!

Love,
Mama

i remember...

when i was

AFRAID

**T**HE AUTHOR

GRATEFULLY ACKNOWLEDGES

THE INSIGHTFUL WISDOM OF

MIKE MORRIS AND CAROL BARTLEY

IN THE REFINING OF THIS CONTENT.

THANK YOU, FRIENDS!

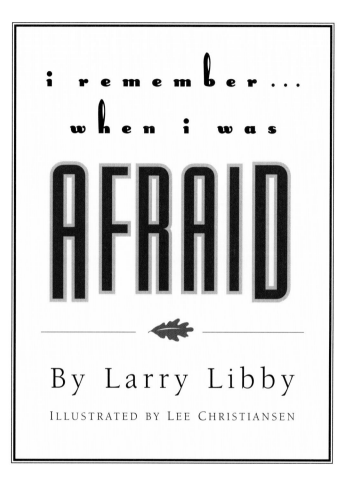

i remember...

when i was

# AFRAID

By Larry Libby

ILLUSTRATED BY LEE CHRISTIANSEN

GOLD 'N' HONEY BOOKS

SISTERS, OREGON

**I Remember…When I Was Afraid**
published by Gold 'n' Honey Books
a part of the Questar publishing family

© 1996 by Questar Publishers, Inc.
Illustrations © 1996 by Lee Christiansen
Designed by David Carlson

International Standard Book Number: 0-88070-919-7

Printed in the United States of America

Most Scripture quotations are from:
The International Children's Bible: New Century Version
© 1986, 1988 by Word Publishing, used by permission.

Scripture references marked SLB are from *The Simplified Living Bible*,
© 1990. Used by permission of Tyndale House Publishers, Inc.
All rights reserved.

Scripture references marked NIV are from The Holy Bible,
New International Version (NIV)
© 1973, 1984 by International Bible Society,
used by permission of Zondervan Publishing House.

Scripture references marked GNB are from
The Good News Bible: The Bible in Today's English Version (TEV)
© 1976 by the American Bible Society.

For information:
Questar Publishers, Inc.
Post Office Box 1720
Sisters, Oregon  97759

Library of Congress Cataloging-in-Publication Data
Libby, Larry
I Remember…When I Was Afraid / Larry Libby.
p.  cm.
Summary: Describes various situations that make people afraid and offers
Bible passages to strengthen our trust in God.
ISBN 0-88070-919-7
1. Fear-Biblical teaching-Juvenile literature.  [1. Fear.
2. Trust in God.]  I. Title
BS680.F4L53  1996
248.8'2--dc20                                              96-1731
                                                            CIP
                                                            AC

96 97 98 99 00 01 02 03 — 10 9 8 7 6 5 4 3 2 1

When I was little, I was scared to death of our old Westinghouse washing machine.

I know it was a strange thing to be afraid of, but…well, this was a strange washing machine.

It had a round window in front. *To me, the window looked like a mouth with rubber jaws.*

It had two dials on top. *To me, the dials looked like eyes.*

The Machine was out in our old, cobwebby garage, and I didn't like to play out there when it was on. It mostly acted like a normal washing machine when it was just washing the clothes (even though it looked to me like it was *chewing* the clothes—with its window-mouth full of sudsy water). But then, when it was through the washing cycle, it suddenly clunked to a stop.

Something clicked inside its oily old gears.

Something winked in its round dial-eyes.

The Machine went into a "spin," and then…it wasn't normal at all. It was angry—crazy—wild. (My dad said it was "out of balance"…and doesn't that *mean* crazy?)

Ker-chunk. Ker-chunk. The spin cycle began slowly at first…with a little shrug and a tremble.

*Ker-chunk—ker-chunk—ker-chunk.* Round and round. Getting faster and faster. And the Machine would shake all over.

*Kerchunk-kerchunk-kerchunk-kerchunk.* Round and round and round and round. Faster and faster and faster. And the Machine would begin to bounce and lurch and jump on its stubby metal legs across the cracked concrete floor…like…it was coming after me…its window-mouth frothing…its dial-eyes glinting in the dim light…its rusty throat-pipe gurgling horribly…its dark underside oozing with oily foam.

One time I got stuck in the garage, just as I heard the "click." The water from the wash cycle began to babble and bubble down the old pipes, and I felt a sort of panic. In only a matter of seconds the machine would go into its terrible spin. I had to move quickly. I ran to the door that opened into the safety of the kitchen, but for some reason, *it was locked.* I pounded and yelled as loud as I could, but no one let me in. *Where was Mom?* I ran to the back door of the garage, but it was stuck (again) on its old warped sill, and I wasn't strong enough to pull it open.

*Mom! Mom!*

Ker-chunk. Ker-chunk.

MOM!

*Ker-chunk—ker-chunk—ker-chunk.*

I was trapped in the garage. Alone.

With the Machine!

*Kerchunk-kerchunk-kerchunk-kerchunk.*

The Machine had me all to itself, but since it was hooked up to all those hoses and wires—like a snarling dog on a short leash—I stayed just out of its reach. I didn't die at all. But boy was I scared! It makes me shudder to think about it. I still get a little edgy walking into a laundromat.

So maybe you think it was crazy to be afraid of an old, out-of-balance washing machine. I guess it was. But I've heard of things just as silly.

I know a little boy who was afraid of the vacuum cleaner. It always made him cry.

I know a little girl who could play with frogs, study spiders right up-close, and admire long, slithery snakes, but was terrified of little white moths landing in her hair.

I know a grown-up lady who was so afraid of thunder she hid in the closet during a thunderstorm. (That's the truth. She really did.)

I know of a big, tall man who was so afraid of sleeping outdoors he never took his family camping—not even once.

I know a grandpa who had been a brave soldier in the war but couldn't stand to ride in a glass-sided elevator in a tall building.

Lots of people are afraid of things, and—even though we may never admit it—most of us are afraid of *something*. Some people are afraid of high places. Some people are afraid of dark places. Some people are afraid of narrow, tight places. Other people are terribly afraid of failing…or trying something new…or being alone…or dying…or even telling other people about Jesus, the One we love most of all.

The Bible has a great deal to say about being afraid. Did you know that? God's Word says clearly that there are some things we *should* be afraid of and other things we should *never* be afraid of. Our fears can keep us from God, but they can also help us grow closer to Him than ever before. And if we find ourselves troubled about these fears of ours, the Bible tells us just what we can do.

Now maybe you're never afraid of anything (or *say* you aren't!). But just in case you ever are or ever were, or just in case you find yourself with someone who is, let's do a little exploring and see what the Bible has to say about all this business of being afraid.

Before we're through, we'll meet some people who *should* have been afraid (but weren't), some other people who *shouldn't* have been afraid (but were), and still other people who *could* have been dreadfully afraid, but found a wonderful way not to be frightened at all.

LOTS OF PEOPLE ARE AFRAID OF THINGS, AND—EVEN THOUGH WE MAY NEVER ADMIT IT— MOST OF US ARE AFRAID OF SOMETHING.

Sometimes I have trouble remembering things. It's not because I'm too old and it's not because I'm too young. It's not that I try to forget…it's just that I don't remember to remember.

When I get excited about something or I'm scooting along on some wild and crazy thought, I can forget all about what I was supposed to do or where I was supposed to be (or even what day it is).

Some people call that being "absent-minded." But my mind isn't absent. It's right there where it always was!

Other people call it "day dreaming." But I'm not dreaming at all. It's just that I'm not thinking about the right things at the right time.

Sometimes being afraid can make us forget things we ought to remember. But if we could only remember just a *little*, it might help us to forget what we were afraid of! Now if you and I were standing too close to a main road and suddenly saw a big gravel truck rumbling toward us in a cloud of dust, we wouldn't have time to do a lot of thinking. It would be time to jump for our lives! In that moment, fear would be God's gift to us to keep us from being hurt.

But mostly, it isn't like that at all.

Usually, when we start to be afraid, we do have time to think about it. We have time to stop for a moment and say to ourselves, *Now, why am I acting this way? Why am I breathing so hard? Why is my heart beating so fast? Why am I so worried? Could I be forgetting something I ought to remember?*

If we slowed ourselves down that much, we might remember to talk to God about whatever is making us afraid. And then God would remind us of all the mighty things He has done for people in the Bible, for people we know, and even for us.

That's just about what Moses told the people of Israel before they moved to their new homes in the Promised Land. Moses knew there were some things in that beautiful new country that might make them afraid. There were castles and forts and armies (and even a few sure-enough giants). God wanted His people to clean those things out of the land as they moved in.

So Moses said:

*You might say to yourselves, "Because these nations are stronger than we are, we can't force them out." But don't be afraid of them. Remember what the LORD your God did to all of Egypt and its king. You saw for yourselves the troubles, signs, and miracles he did, how the LORD'S great power and strength brought you out of Egypt.… Don't be afraid of them, because the LORD your God is with you;*

*he is a great God and people are afraid of him.*
(Deuteronomy 7:17-19, 21)

I *like* those words, don't you?

It's as if Moses were saying, "Okay, there you are, little soldier…marching, marching up to the huge gates of a great enemy fort. And there are giants on the wall above you, howling at you, scowling at you, and getting ready to throw watermelon-sized boulders at you or shoot arrows at you or whatever it is mean giants like to do.

"Now, little soldier, you have a funny feeling in your stomach. Your legs feel kind of wobbly. Your heart is beating fast. You've never been in this kind of fix before. You feel like turning around and running away as fast as you can! But stop and remember, little soldier…. Remember what a BIG God you have. Remember all the amazing and powerful things this BIG God has made and done. Remember how much this BIG God loves you and watches over you. Think about *those* things, little soldier, and you won't be afraid anymore!"

Those are such good thoughts, I really don't want to forget them. Maybe we could help each other remember to remember to remember them!

The rest of this book may do just that.

## the very first thing to do (when you are afraid)

In any real emergency, the first thing to do is find a phone, call 9-1-1, and explain your need for help.

But we can't call 9-1-1 for just being afraid! So what is the very first thing we should do when we're afraid? I love the story about what one king did on the scariest day of his whole life.

The Bible tells us that three powerful armies had united to attack King Jehoshaphat and his tiny kingdom of Judah.

*Messengers came and told Jehoshaphat, "A large army is coming against you from Edom, from the other side of the Dead Sea." …Jehoshaphat was afraid, so he decided to ask the LORD what to do. He announced that no one in Judah should eat during this special time of prayer to God. The people of Judah came together to ask the LORD for help; they came from every town in Judah.*

*…Then Jehoshaphat stood up, and he said, "LORD, God of our ancestors, you are the God in heaven. You rule over all the kingdoms of the nations.*

*You have power and strength, so no one can stand
against you....*

*"We have no power against this large army that
is attacking us. We don't know what to do, so we look
to you for help."*
(2 Chronicles 20:2-6, 12)

What a wise decision King Jehoshaphat made!
He was afraid, yes. Very afraid.

And with good reason! A vast army, with more
soldiers than anyone could count, was marching
toward his little country—closer every minute. If you
could have been in an airplane and seen those soldiers, they would have looked like an army of ants
covering the hills and the valleys—creeping toward
Jerusalem like a dark shadow.

The king might have done several things
when he was so afraid, but here are some things he
*didn't* do.

He didn't lie to himself and pretend everything
    was okay. (It wasn't.)

He didn't run away.

He didn't blame other people.

He didn't hide.

He didn't moan and cry.

He didn't yell at his wife and kids and
    kick the dog.

He didn't sit frozen like a statue on his throne.

He didn't crouch in a corner and sulk.

What did that good king do? He took his fear to
God! Right away! *The very first thing* he did was to ask
the Lord for help. The very first place he went was to
his knees. And he didn't pray alone, either. He called
everybody in his whole country to what must have
been the biggest prayer meeting ever—and they all
came. (That's the handy part about being a king.)

*Just listen to who came to the king's prayer meeting.
All of the men of Judah stood before the* LORD *with
their babies, wives, and children.* (20:13)

Everybody came! Dads and moms. Big brothers
and little sisters. Grown-up sisters and baby brothers.
Aunts and uncles and cousins and grandpas and
grandmas. They all came at this very scary time to
pray with their king.

Do you see? Being afraid can be a good thing.
Everybody in a whole country got together and
prayed to the Lord. Everybody—young and old, men
and women, boys and girls, rich and poor—turned
to the Lord for help. I think it would help our
country to be afraid for a while, don't you?

I love the way this good king prayed. He was
saying, *Oh, Lord, we're scared of this big army! But You
are bigger than anyone. This enemy is too strong for us.
But You are stronger than anyone. We can't face this problem alone, and we don't even know what to do next! But
here we are, all together, and we're asking You for help.*

God loves to answer that kind of prayer. And He
answered right away. As soon as the king was through
praying, the Lord spoke a message to one of His

"WE DON'T KNOW
WHAT TO DO,
SO WE LOOK TO
YOU FOR HELP."
2 CHRONICLES
20:12

special servants, and this is what the message said:

*"Don't be afraid or discouraged because of this large army. The battle is not your battle, it is God's.... You won't need to fight in this battle. Just stand strong in your places, and you will see the LORD save you. Judah and Jerusalem, don't be afraid or discouraged, because the LORD is with you."* (20:15, 17)

And before the sun set on the next day, God caused that enemy army to fight against *each other*. All the enemy soldiers died, and not one of God's people had to fight. Judah's army never needed a single Band-Aid.

Tell me…what is the very first thing you do when you are afraid?

Do you run?

Hide? Cry?

Get mad?

Pull the covers over your head?

Fake it and pretend you feel fine?

If you could go for a little walk with good King Jehoshaphat, he might tell you, "Don't wait! Don't stop to worry! Run to God as fast as you can."

That's what *he* did, and what a good choice that was. As it turns out, the best battle he ever fought was one he never had to fight at all.

# fear is like a trap

o you want to hear something really strange?

There are times when I worry more about what *people* think about me than what *God* thinks about me.

Now why is that? I know that pleasing God is much more important than pleasing anyone else. I know that God loves and cares about me more than anyone else.

I also know God is much more powerful than anyone else.

So what makes me more afraid of "Anyone Else" than I am of HIM?

I've wondered about that. And here's what I think. God is invisible to my eyes, and they aren't! I can see their faces. I can hear their words. I can see them frowning at me if they are angry. I can hear them laughing if they're making fun of me. It's easy to think about them because God seems far away (somewhere off in Heaven) while they are right there in front of me.

When we start to feel that way, we need to remember God's Word. God's Word says He is not far away from us, He is near! Nearer than anyone else! He is close. He is concerned. He watches everything we do. He listens to everything we say. He knows every thought we think. He expects us to obey Him, no matter what other people might do or say to us.

The Bible tells us,
*Fear of man will prove to be a snare, but whoever trusts in the LORD is kept safe.*
(Proverbs 29:25, NIV)

Do you know what a "snare" is?

It's a trap!

Imagine you were trying to snare a rabbit. How would you do it?

Well…you might prop up a heavy wooden box with a stick. You might put a crisp, fresh carrot inside the box, tie a string to your prop, and then hide yourself behind a tree to watch. Then, when that rabbit hopped over to sniff at that delicious-smelling treat—ZING!—you'd pull on the string and—THUMP!—the box would fall over the rabbit, and you'd have him prisoner. (Poor ol' bunny!)

The Bible says that being afraid of what people think or what people will do is like stepping into a snare. ZING! THUMP! The line goes tight, the box falls, and you are *trapped*. What's it like when you're trapped?

You can't go forward.

You can't go backward.

You can't get away.

You can't do what you want to do anymore. Your fear has you tangled up and boxed in.

How do you keep out of snares? (No, it's not by staying away from carrots!) The Bible says you are safe when you trust the Lord. You are safe when what you care about most is pleasing Him—*no matter what other people say or do*. You are safe when you make sure that obeying the Lord is the very first thing you get done.

But it isn't easy!

Even great, important men and women have gotten themselves tangled up in that old Fear-of-People Snare. Israel's very first king—a tall, strong, handsome man named Saul—got into the worst kind of trouble over fear of what people were thinking about him. He disobeyed the Lord's clear command, and God's prophet Samuel was very angry over what the king had done. But Saul had no excuse. With a sad, red face, he mumbled these words to Samuel:

*"I have sinned. I didn't obey the LORD'S commands and your words. I was afraid of the people, and I did what they said."* (1 Samuel 15:24)

Saul got caught in the snare! Like a mouse in a trap. Like a fly in a web. Like a fish in a net. Like a bunny in a box. And the sad thing was, he never, ever got out. Not in a week. Not in a year. He was snarled up for the rest of his life. God and Samuel had to look for a new king to take Saul's place, and that's when they found a shepherd boy named David. (But that's another story!)

How can you and I keep away from snares that try to trip us and tangle our feet? How can we keep from worrying about "what people think" instead of trusting the Lord? Well, maybe the best thing to do is just to ask God for help.

I could say a prayer like this:

Lord, You know I'm starting to feel afraid. I'm afraid of what other people will say about me. I'm afraid of what other people might do to me. I can't stop thinking about it. Dear Lord, please help those people to grow *very little* in my mind while You grow *very big*. I pray that they will grow so little and that You will grow so big that I won't be able to even see them anymore. I want my eyes to be filled with You, instead. Please keep my feet out of traps and snares, Lord, because I want to run and laugh and sing and not be tied up or boxed in or afraid. In Jesus' strong name I pray, Amen.

## he is with me

Sometimes dads and moms take their kids to some pretty scary places.

Has your family ever stopped to look over the edge of a deep canyon with a river down below? The river is so far away it looks like a shiny, silver-blue ribbon winding along the bottom.

Has your family ever driven through the mountains where the car gets so close to the edge that you can see way, way down below you? Sometimes, you can look *down* and see clouds—and birds flying around!

Have you ever sat with your mom or dad in an airplane when it started bouncing and shaking in a stormy sky?

Have you ever walked down a road at night with your mom or dad when the wind is making dead leaves skitter along the ground, the tree branches creak and groan, and ragged clouds are flying past the moon?

It would be frightening to be in those places all alone. And it's just a *little bit* scary to be there with your mom or dad. But not very much! Why? Because Dad is *with* you. Because Mom is *with* you.

That's what David said about a place he called "the valley of the shadow of death."

*Even though I walk*

*through the valley of the shadow of death,*

*I will fear no evil,*

*for you are with me.*

(Psalm 23:4, NIV)

This was a road David didn't want to walk.

This was a place David didn't want to be.

It was a dark place where he couldn't see the blue sky. It was a cold place where he couldn't feel the warmth of the sun. It was a strange place where he didn't know what was around the next corner. David was afraid of that place. David would rather have been any other place in the whole world.

But there was nothing he could do about it! His path led right down into that land of shadows. And even though his feet didn't want to go down there, he reached up, felt for the Lord's big hand, took a deep breath, and off he went.

But do you know what he said as he started on his way?

"Even if I have to walk through that dark, gloomy valley—I won't fear! Because I know *You* are with me, Lord! And if *You* are with me, nothing can make me afraid."

I agree with David!

No valley in all the wide world is "too dark" if God is there with me.

It is better—so much better—to walk in a narrow canyon of shadows *with God* than to stand in a bright field of flowers…without Him.

It is better—so very much better—to crouch under a leafless tree in a cold rain *with God* than to walk golden sands by a calm, blue ocean… without Him.

It is better—I can't tell you how much better—to be in a dark, scary, lonely place *with God* than to be in a warm, safe, sunny place…without Him.

David knew that even when it came time to die—even when he came to that darkest of all valleys—he had no reason to be afraid at all. Why? Because God was still with him.

God would never let go of his hand. Not even for a minute.

And God won't let go of your hand, either. Will you say the words out loud with me now?

*He is with me!*

## seeing how god sees

Down on your stomach with your face right close to the ground (the way an ant might see things), the world looks very different. Have you ever tried it?

Get down as low as you can, and then look around at the world. Grass and weeds and flowers look tall as trees. Way down low like that…

a kitten could look like a huge tiger,

a lizard could look like a tyrannosaurus,

a worm could look like a giant snake,

a beetle could look like a movie monster.

But then, when you get off your stomach and stand up again, those little things don't look big any-more, do they? They look their own true size. And of course there's no reason to fear a kitten or a lizard or a worm or a beetle. (I do know of one grown-up lady who isn't fond of beetles. No, not at all.)

Sometimes scientists look at unbelievably tiny creatures under powerful microscopes. And as they peer down at those smallest of living things—so much smaller than a grain of salt or a flake of dust—the creatures look like huge, horrible monsters with bulging eyes and thrashing tails and snapping jaws. Some of God's tiniest creatures live in drops of water, or on the stems of plants.

They even live in your eyebrows!

WHO HAS

MEASURED THE

OCEANS IN

THE PALM OF

HIS HAND?

WHO HAS USED

HIS HAND TO

MEASURE

THE SKY?

ISAIAH 40:12

Do you think those men and women are afraid of what they see in their microscopes? Not a bit! Now if they ever met creatures like that sneaking over their back fence at night, they might be. But these scientists know that those frightful-looking "monsters" are really so incredibly tiny they could never bother anybody. Even a flea wouldn't pay any attention to them or guess that they were there.

In the same way, the things that look so huge and frightening to you and me aren't huge or frightening at all to God. Sometimes you and I forget just how great and awesome our God really is. Listen to what the Bible says about Him—and use your *imagination* as you read these words!

> *Who has measured the oceans in the palm*
> *of his hand?*
> *Who has used his hand to measure*
> *the sky?*
> *Who has used a bowl to measure all the*
> *dust of the earth and scales to weigh*
> *the mountains and hills?*
> *…The nations are like one small drop*
> *in a bucket;*
> *they are no more than the dust on his*
> *measuring scales….*
> *Have you not heard how the world began?*
> *It was made by the one who sits on his*
> *throne above the earth and beyond the sky;*
> *the people below look as tiny as ants.*

> *He stretched out the sky like a curtain, like a*
> *tent in which to live.*

(Isaiah 40:12, 15; Isaiah 40:21-22, GNB)

This mighty Creator-God of ours sees things as they really are and has never been frightened of anything or anybody.

Once there was a king named Ahaz, who was terribly afraid of two neighbor kings. As he walked the walls around his city, his eyes would stray toward the horizon in the north and his shoulders would give a little shudder. As he sat in his banquet hall picking nervously at his dinner, he felt sure someone would come running in at any moment and start wailing, "Oh, no! Oh, help! All is lost! Here come the Syrians! Here come the Israelites!"

When would those enemy kings attack? Would they kill everybody? Would they make him a prisoner? How could he hope to stop them? That's just about all King Ahaz could think about. He knew their armies were large and powerful and his army wasn't. So he was afraid all the time.

He was afraid when he went to bed at night.

He was afraid when he woke up in the morning.

He was afraid when he strolled in his royal garden and afraid when he brushed his royal teeth. What a miserable way to live! Here's how the Bible tells this true story:

> *Ahaz king of Judah received a message saying, "The*
> *armies of Aram and Israel have joined together."*

*When Ahaz heard this, he and the people were frightened. They shook with fear like the trees of the forest blown by the wind.* (Isaiah 7:2-3)

Have you ever been in the woods when the wind started to blow very hard? Do you remember what it sounded like as the leaves madly rattled and tree limbs banged together? That's what it must have sounded like in that little kingdom of Judah. You could hear teeth chattering and knees knocking across the whole land. And no knees knocked any harder than the knees of that timid, trembling king named Ahaz.

God knew how frightened King Ahaz was. (It's no use to trying to hide it from God. He knows you are afraid even before you do.) So God sent His special messenger to Ahaz with these surprising words:

*"Tell Ahaz, 'Be careful. Be calm and don't worry. Don't let those two [kings] scare you. Don't be afraid of their anger or Aram's anger, because they are like two barely burning sticks that are ready to go out.'"* (Isaiah 7:4)

Burning sticks! Do you know what that makes me think of?

Matches!

Have you ever watched someone light a match? Sometimes dads use about ten thousand of them trying to get the barbecue grill lit. Just for a second, the match goes *whooosh* and a little flame jumps up. Then what happens? The flame burns yellow for a moment and then turns weak and blue-ish. After a few seconds—and usually before it can do any good—out it goes in a little puff of smoke. (Don't you try this! You might start a dangerous fire where you don't want one!)

"That's what these two kings look like to Me," God was saying to Ahaz. "They look like a couple of matches that spark for a moment. And then all I have to do is blow on them—just give them a little puff—and out they go! Oh Ahaz, don't be afraid of a couple of puny matches. These kings aren't as hot as they think they are!"

But Ahaz wasn't ready to believe the Lord. Instead of holding on to the Lord's good words, he held on to his fear. To him, the two kings looked like huge forest fires burning on the northern horizon. But really, it was like being on your stomach and looking at a beetle. He needed to stand up like a true king and see things the way they really were, didn't he? He needed to see his enemies through God's eyes, and he wouldn't have been afraid anymore.

Only the Lord can help us to stand tall and see things the way He sees things.

How can you stand tall if you're too short? Well, that's easy. Ask Him for a boost!

**E**lijah was sitting all by himself on top of a small hill, and he wasn't about to come down.

Now if you had been Elijah, you wouldn't have wanted to come down, either. The top of a hill is not such a bad place to spend a sunny afternoon—especially if there are fifty soldiers at the bottom of the hill waiting to take you where you don't want to go.

These were soldiers of the evil King Ahaziah, and they weren't there to sell cookies to Elijah or play Monopoly with him. The king and his soldiers hated Elijah because he was God's man, and you can be sure they wanted to hurt him.

As you might imagine, when Elijah saw those soldiers march up to his hill with the morning sun glinting off their swords and helmets, he was afraid. The top of that hill looked like a fine place to stay (if only he'd remembered to pack a couple of peanut butter sandwiches and a sleeping bag).

But just then the Lord's angel came to visit Elijah up on that little hilltop.

*The LORD'S angel said to Elijah, "Go down with [the captain] and don't be afraid of him." So Elijah got up and went down with him to see the king.*
(2 Kings 1:15)

Suddenly the top of that hill didn't look like such a great place to stay after all. When God tells you to move, where you are is never a good place to stay— no matter how comfortable and safe and homey it might seem. The best place you and I could ever be is right where God wants us to be—no matter how fearful or puzzling or uncomfortable it might look at the time.

So Elijah was ready to go with the fifty soldiers— or a hundred soldiers—or a thousand soldiers. It didn't matter how many soldiers were waiting at the bottom of that little hill because God's own angel had told him it was okay.

And the angel also told him, "Don't be afraid."

Angels are always saying that. It's usually the very first thing they do say.

I can't help wondering if suddenly seeing an angel on that hilltop frightened Elijah almost as much as the soldiers had. Oh sure, Elijah had seen angels before. He'd even had an angel serve him breakfast under a bush once (but that's another story).

Still…you have to wonder. Does anyone ever get used to seeing an angel?

It has always seemed strange to me that God sends *angels* to tell people not to be afraid—when just seeing an angel seems to scare most folks half out of their wits.

I keep thinking about the angel who told Daniel not to be afraid. Oh, but Daniel was afraid! When the powerful angel suddenly appeared beside him on the river bank, Daniel felt like he was going to die of fright. If there had been a gopher hole nearby, I'm sure Daniel would have tried to squeeze into it. Here is what he wrote about that moment:

*I lost my strength, my face turned white like a dead person, and I was helpless….*

*I fell into a deep sleep with my face on the ground.*

*Then a hand touched me and set me on my hands and knees. I was so afraid that I was shaking…. I stood up, but I was still shaking.*

(Daniel 10:8-11)

And what did the angel say to Daniel?

*"Daniel, don't be afraid. God loves you very much. Peace be with you. Be strong now; be courageous."*

(Daniel 10:19)

That was easy for the angel to *say*, but not so easy for Daniel to *do!*

Sometimes I imagine there must be a school in Heaven for angels. What might an angel need to learn?

How to fly faster than a shooting star?

How to fight the devil's dark angels?

How to carry God's messages

(and get them right every time)?

If there were such a school for angels, I'll bet I know one lesson every single angel student would study—

"DANIEL, DON'T BE AFRAID. GOD LOVES YOU VERY MUCH. PEACE BE WITH YOU. BE STRONG NOW; BE COURAGEOUS."

DANIEL 10:19

"When you visit Earth and talk to people there, you are probably going to scare them so badly they will faint. So the thing you have to do right away is say, 'Don't be afraid.'"

I can just imagine the angel teacher working with his angel students. And the angel teacher says, "All right, class (you're all being *such* angels today), let's practice our lesson together. Ready?… 'Don't be afraid!'"

And the angels all say together, *"Don't be afraid."*

"Don't what?"

*"Don't be afraid."*

"I can't hear you!"

"DON'T BE AFRAID!"

But of course it almost never works. Even though the angels are careful to remember their lines and say "Don't be afraid" just as soon as they pop into a room, most everybody is afraid anyway. Well, wouldn't *you* be?

After all, angels can't help looking so bright and mighty and other-worldly. That's just the way they are! And they can't help popping in and out of places. That's just the way they travel. If you were an angel, you would pop in and out, too. We might wish they would ring the doorbell, tap politely on our door, or call us first from a pay phone to give us a little warning. But that's just not the way angels work. When God gives them a message to carry, they're so eager to obey and please Him they *leap* into the job with all their hearts. (We could learn a lot from angels.)

I'm telling you this so that if an angel pops into *your* room sometime, you won't be too startled. And one of the things an angel might tell you (right off the bat) is not to be afraid of something that *has* been making you afraid. If that's what he tells you, you can believe it!

I'm glad God knows all about us. I'm glad He understands when we're troubled or afraid. Even if the thing we're afraid of might seem silly to other people (like washing machines or moths or elevators), it's not silly to God! When God whispers to me or you that we don't need to be afraid, then we can trust Him and relax.

But just between you and me, I'd rather He didn't send an angel with the message.

**N**o one had lived in the city of Jerusalem for many long years.

There was no place to live! God had allowed His special city to be completely smashed down and burned up by enemies because of His people's disobedience and sin. God had sent warning after warning. God's servants the prophets had pleaded with the people for years to turn back to the Lord.

But no one would listen. No one paid any attention to God's warnings. And finally the enemy soldiers swept over Jerusalem like a violent storm out of the dark north.

Many people died, but many more were marched away as captives to the faraway country of Babylon. Nothing much was left of Jerusalem but jagged pieces of wall, some eerie-looking caved-in buildings, and piles of fire-blackened rubble.

Now, all the owls, sparrows, rats, bats, foxes, and other wild creatures thought this situation was just fine. They liked it better with the people gone. They liked having the streets overgrown with weeds and brush. They liked burrowing under the tumbled-down walls or nesting in the burned-out houses or skittering around in the rubble-choked basements. It was quiet and peaceful—in a lonely sort of way—with only the sound of the wind whistling around rock piles and through dark, empty windows.

The ruined city of Jerusalem didn't miss God's people at all. But God's people missed Jerusalem!

So after years and years, when they finally had the chance, a group of God's people decided to head home. They moved their families back to that once-beautiful city, to worship the Lord as their grandparents and great-grandparents had done.

The first thing they wanted to do when they got there was to start building an altar to the Lord. They did this because God's Word had said that's the way they should worship—and they wanted to please Him!

But there was one problem. A big problem. The people who were now living around the burned-out city didn't *want* God's people coming back. They didn't want Jerusalem rebuilt. And since they didn't love God, they certainly didn't want anyone worshiping the Lord at a new altar!

This little band of God's people were outnumbered and surrounded by God's enemies who didn't want them to be there and who watched every move they made! If they even started to work on that altar, they could be attacked. They could be taken prisoner. They could be wounded. They could be killed.

So what did they do?

What would *you* do?

They *so* much wanted to obey the Lord, but so many people were against them! Do you think they packed up and went back to Babylon? Do you think they decided to "put off" building an altar (and maybe built a library or a chariot-wash instead)? The Bible tells us what happened next:

*[They] began to build the altar of the God of Israel where they could offer burnt offerings, just as it is written in the Teachings of Moses, the man of God. Even though they were afraid of the people living around them, they built the altar where it had been before. And they offered burnt offerings on it to the* LORD *morning and evening.* (Ezra 3:2-3)

They had fear in their hearts. But they did the right thing anyway!

Their throats felt tight and their knees felt weak and their hands felt trembly. But they kept right on doing what God wanted.

They were nervous and worried about what might happen to them. But they pushed those worries aside, took a deep breath, rolled up their sleeves, and got busy with the work at hand.

They were afraid of making their enemies angry. But they were even *more* afraid of displeasing their God!

Doing the *right* thing isn't always the *easy* thing, is it? Obeying the Lord can even be scary sometimes. The work may be hard. Others may not like what we're doing or how we're doing it. God's enemies may

threaten us, bully us, or try to make the courage melt right out of our hearts. People who don't understand and don't *want* to understand may tell us we're nothing but silly fools.

But the Bible tells us: *Obey anyway!*

Obey God even when you're afraid and don't know what might happen next. Do the right thing even when others say you shouldn't or couldn't. Follow the Lord even when everyone else seems to be giving up and going the other way.

There will still be days (or nights!) when we feel afraid. After all, feelings come and go, like wind that pushes a kite this way and that. But sometimes the best thing to do with feelings is just to start out walking in the right direction and let them tag along behind. (They *will* catch up, sooner or later.)

It's better to obey God—even with deep fear in our hearts—than to think about staying safe and comfortable. After all, walking close to Him is the safest place anyone could ever be!

## scaring people isn't hard

When you stop to think about it, most people scare pretty easily.

We humans are a jumpy bunch of folks. God knows that very well, of course, and He doesn't frighten us unless we *need* to be frightened for our own good. If God ever wanted to scare us—really scare us—oh, my—just think of the job He could do! But He isn't that way at all, is He? What God likes to do is help frightened people find Him and trust Him.

If people were more like God, they wouldn't be trying to scare one another. They would be trying to help each other trust the Lord, instead.

For some reason, my big brothers always liked to scare me when I was a little boy. Especially when we were camping.

Sometime after the campfire had burned down to shimmery red embers…and the first stars were peeking through the purple twilight…after roasting a few marshmallows a nice golden brown (and burning about ten more into black, crusty blobs), it would be time to crawl into the cozy tent and zip up tight in the old sleeping bag.

Or—almost time.

I usually wanted to make one last trip to the little outhouse. When you're camping, of course, the bathroom isn't in some nice lighted room right down the hall! You have to find the little trail and take a bit of a walk before you get where you want to go.

That was no problem during the day. But I didn't like it much at night.

Things look different in the dark. Have you noticed that?

Trails look different in the dark.

Trees look different in the dark.

Plain old stumps can turn into crouching bears. A tree branch at the side of the trail can turn into a bony hand that tries to tickle your neck or grab your shirt from behind. Shadows leap, lurch, and stretch at the edge of a flashlight beam.

I didn't really want to go down the trail in the dark, but I *had* to go down that trail (if you know what I mean). My brothers would see me heading off in that direction, look at each other, and smile. Then they would run ahead of me and hide behind some trees. When I came down the path, feeling my way along in the spooky dark with my little flashlight, they would jump out and yell, "YAAAAAAA!"

Now I *really* hated that.

Even though I knew they might do something like that, it almost always gave me a heart attack. And it would make me yell, too. "AAAAUUUGGGHHH!"

I always jumped. I always yelled. I always got mad. I don't know why, but big brothers just *love* that kind of stuff.

No, scaring people isn't hard at all. At certain times and at certain places, almost anyone can scare anyone else.

There's something that's a lot harder than scaring people. Do you know what it is?

The hard thing is to help somebody to not be afraid. The hard thing is to make frightened people feel brave! Have you ever done THAT? If you have, you know what a tough job it can be (and how good it feels when you really manage to do it).

That's the very job Caleb and Joshua had when they got back from their spying trip to the Promised Land. And it was just about the hardest job they ever had.

Do you remember that story? All of God's people—millions of them—were camped together in the desert, waiting for their chance to go in to the beautiful land God had told them about. But first, Moses sent twelve spies into that country to see what it was like.

This was their report:

*"We came to the land you sent us to see. It is indeed a wonderful country! It is a land 'flowing with milk and honey.' Here is some fruit we have brought as proof. But the people living there are powerful. Their cities have walls around them, and they are very large. What's more, we saw Anakim giants there!…"*

But Caleb reassured the people as they stood before Moses. *"Let us go up at once and possess it!"* he said. *"For we are well able to conquer it."*

*"Not against people as strong as they are!"* the other spies said. *"They would crush us!"*

*So most of the spies were afraid. "The land is full of warriors," they said. "The people are too strong. We saw some of the Anakim there. They came from the ancient race of giants. We felt like grasshoppers beside them. They were so tall!"*

*Then all the people began weeping aloud. They carried on all night. Their voices rose in a great chorus of complaint against Moses and Aaron.*
(Numbers 13:27-28, 30-33; 14:1-2, SLB)

You see, even though there were two men who believed God and tried to help people not to be afraid, there were TEN men who did not believe God and made the people very afraid. And do you know what being afraid caused them to do? It caused them to cry and complain and disobey the Lord. Many years later, when Joshua was an old man, he remembered that sad, terrible day. And this is what he said:

*"But my brothers who went up with me made the hearts of the people melt with fear. I, however,* *followed the LORD my God wholeheartedly."*
(Joshua 14:8, NIV)

You and I can be the sort of people who make others afraid…or we can be the sort of people who help others trust God and not be afraid.

We can say the kind of words that frighten people and make them worried…or we can say the kind of words that give people fresh courage and help them remember their strong, loving Lord.

We can be like the ten men who sat in camp and fussed and sniffled and chewed on their fingernails…or like the two men who said, "God's with us! We can do it! Hey, let's go for it!"

*Anybody* can make someone afraid. A dog can do that. A junior-sized spider can do that. An old rotten stump sitting in the dark can do that. But helping someone to be strong and trust God like Joshua and Caleb…well, that's a bigger and harder job.

But I think I'd like to give it a try.
How about you?

# when fear is a gift from god

Do you have curtains on your windows at home? Curtains are helpful at night. When we close them they keep people from looking in our windows.

But who wants to keep the curtains closed in the daytime? Not me! I want to see miles and miles of blue sky. I want to see rain puddles painted by sunsets and grass flashing with dew diamonds and even solemn gray clouds huddling before a storm. I want to see a cat chasing a leaf and a robin chasing a worm and sunlight chasing a shadow.

Did you know that some people live most of their lives without ever seeing what God has done? It's as though thick curtains are closed over their hearts—day and night—making it dark inside.

They close their eyes to things that show God's endless power.

They close their minds to the truth of God's pure and beautiful wisdom.

They close their hearts to the story of God's strong love.

They get up in the mornings and feel God's sunshine on their faces. They sit at breakfast and eat cereal grown in God's fields and drink juice from fruit grown on God's trees. They look out their windows at work or school and see God's clouds sailing like great ships across His wide heavens.

But all the time, they pretend there is no God. They don't give Him thanks. They don't obey His commands. They don't believe His wondrous Word. They don't care about His love. They're not afraid of His mighty power or His punishment.

It's as if they are living behind heavy curtains and can't see!

But do you know what *fear* can do? Fear can suddenly jerk back the curtains on people's hearts. And in that moment when the curtains are pulled back, God's Holy Spirit can show them the truth!

Fear helps them to open their eyes and see what they might not have seen before.

For that reason, being afraid could be the best gift a person could ever receive.

Because of His love, God may allow something to come crashing into the lives of these people to make them afraid. God knows there is a chance that when they are most afraid, they may peek at the *real* world outside their curtains. They might turn to Him and become His children through all the glad, shining days of forever.

Have you ever noticed that when people are suddenly afraid, they will sometimes yell out the name of God or Jesus? Now maybe they are just

swearing. But when their life is in danger, or their world is shaken, they suddenly think about God—and know in their hearts that they need Him!

Did you know that the man who judged Jesus and sent Him to die on a cross was afraid? God sent Him that fear. *If only he had listened to it!*

*The judge named Pilate was standing with Jesus in front of an angry crowd of people.*

*When the leading priests and the guards saw Jesus, they shouted, "Crucify him! Crucify him!"*

*But Pilate answered, "Crucify him yourselves, because I find nothing against him."*

*The Jews answered, "We have a law that says he should die, because he said he is the Son of God."*

*When Pilate heard this, he was even more afraid.* (John 19:6-8)

Pilate was right to be afraid! Something in his heart told him that Jesus just might be more than a man. He just might be *the Son of Almighty God.*

While Pilate was trying to make up his mind what to do, somebody handed him a note that made him more afraid than ever. The note was from Mrs. Pilate!

*While Pilate was sitting there on the judge's seat, his wife sent this message to him: "Don't do anything to that man, because he is innocent. Today I had a dream about him, and it troubled me very much."* (Matthew 27:19)

How God loved this weak, fearful judge! But even though Pilate came very close to hearing God's voice in his fear, in the end he closed his eyes and ears again. In the end, he pulled the black curtains tight around his heart. In the end, he was more afraid of the people than he was of God. So on that saddest of all days, Judge Pilate gave Jesus to the soldiers who would kill Him. Pilate went home that night to hear his wife say, "Didn't you get my note? Didn't you hear my warning?" But it was too late. As far as we know (which isn't so very far), Pilate never found God at all.

Years later, another man from Rome, named Felix, also heard God call to him in his fear. Felix was a governor, and he came to listen to the apostle Paul, who had been held prisoner for telling people about Jesus. Here's what happened.

*After some days Felix came…and asked for Paul to be brought to him. He listened to Paul talk about believing in Christ Jesus. But Felix became afraid when Paul spoke about living right, self-control, and the time when God will judge the world. He said, "Go away now. When I have more time, I will call for you."* (Acts 24:24-25)

But Felix wasn't telling the truth. He was lying to Paul, and he was lying to himself, too. He would *never* find a better time to hear about God's love and salvation. (The best time you could ever find Jesus as your Savior is always *right now.*) Governor Felix should have listened to the fear in his heart and turned to the Lord.

But he didn't. He said, "Go away, Paul. This talk makes me nervous. I'll think about it some other time." But as far as we know, there never was another time for Felix, and he never found God's love and forgiveness.

When I was a nine-year-old boy, I became very afraid of not going to Heaven. I was afraid that when I died, God would shut Heaven's door and leave me outside in the dark—forever. I was so afraid I couldn't sleep very well at night. And when I did sleep, I had nightmares.

Now, you could say it wasn't good for a boy to be so afraid. It's true that there was a lot I didn't understand. But do you know what that fear in my heart led me to do? I asked Jesus to be my Savior. I let that fear inside me push me right into God's strong arms. And in that very moment, I became God's own child…and little by little, He began to take my fear away.

Being afraid of missing Heaven is a right thing to be afraid of! If that fear pushes you into the safe-keeping arms of God, then it is the best gift you'll ever receive!

## fear & joy

Can a person be happy and afraid—all at the same time?

That would be like feeling hot and cold at the same time. Or up and down. Or in and out. Or wet and dry. You're either one or the other…aren't you?

But the Bible says we really can be happy and afraid at the same time. And then it tells us about a couple of women who were! Both of them were named "Mary," both of them loved the Lord Jesus, and both of them learned what it meant to be terribly afraid—and spilling over with gladness and laughter all on the same astonishing morning.

It was a still Sunday morning, just before sunrise.

Do you know what it's like outside before the sun comes up? The light in the east is still dim, soft as the glow of a night light in a dark room. The stars seem to grow smaller and farther away as you watch them, until they're like tiny silver pins stuck into an inky sky. The moonlight seems tired and slips slowly away—like an old man shuffling into the distance with a pale lantern.

It's a time of day when trails are dim, faces are shadowed, and everyday places seem unfamiliar and strange. But that's when these two Marys walked together down a lonely path to a sad place.

They were going to a grave.

They wanted to find the new tomb of their Lord and Friend, Jesus. They wanted to look at the place where some men had laid His dead body.

Yes, they knew Jesus was dead. They knew He had been killed on a cross by hateful men. They knew they could no longer hear His voice or feel His touch or look into His kind, loving eyes. But still…they wanted to be close to His body. They wanted to see what kind of place He was buried in.

Why did they get up so early to go to that tomb carved in the rock? Maybe it was because they were afraid of those who had killed Jesus. Maybe it was because they'd been crying all night long and couldn't sleep.

Or maybe it was because of the earthquake!

Because some time early that Sunday morning a violent earthquake shook all the houses down to their foundations, all the trees down to their roots, and all the people down to their bones. Here is what the Bible says about it:

*At that time there was a strong earthquake. An angel of the Lord came down from heaven, went to the tomb, and rolled the stone away from the entrance. Then he sat on the stone. He was shining as bright as lightning, and his clothes were white as snow.* (Matthew 28:2-3)

When the two Marys got to the grave, there was the angel, shining brighter than the sun just edging up over the horizon. It was like being between two sunrises, and they were dazed and dazzled! The tomb in the rock was open, the soldiers guarding it were gone, and *no one was inside!*

The angel spoke to them, and what do you suppose his voice was like that Sunday morning? Like thunder in the mountains? Like golden music dancing on a sunrise? Like a sudden, joyful wind racing through the treetops?

*The angel said to the women, "Don't be afraid. I know that you are looking for Jesus, who has been crucified. He is not here. He has risen from the dead as he said he would. Come and see the place where his body was. And go quickly and tell his followers, 'Jesus has risen from the dead.'"*
(Matthew 28:5-7)

Of course the women did just what the angel had said. Who wants to stand there arguing with an angel when the sun is up and the grave is empty and the Lord is somewhere ALIVE! Listen now to what the Bible says happened next:

*So the women hurried away from the tomb, afraid yet filled with joy, and ran to tell his disciples. Suddenly Jesus met them. "Greetings," he said. They came to him, clasped his feet and worshiped him. Then Jesus said to them, "Do not be afraid."*
(Matthew 28:8-10, NIV)

THOSE LIVING

FAR AWAY FEAR

YOUR WONDERS;

WHERE MORNING

DAWNS AND

EVENING FADES

YOU CALL

FORTH SONGS

OF JOY.

PSALM 65:8

This was a time when fear was mixed with wonder. This was a time when darkness was shattered by light. This was a time when heavy sadness fell away like an old winter coat and swift, sure joy rushed in with the new morning.

That's the way it is with God sometimes when He works wonders. He's so vast, and blinding-bright, and powerful-beyond-imagination that we could be afraid of Him. But this isn't like being afraid of something evil or cruel or mean. This isn't like fear of a bully that's all mixed up with anger and shame. This is a kind of fear that has joy pushing behind it and shining all around its edges. Why? Because we know that this mighty, sometimes frightening, awesome God loves us and cares for us.

When David thought about this, he wrote:
Those living far away fear your wonders;
where morning dawns and evening fades

you call forth songs of joy. (Psalm 65:8, NIV)

When morning dawned for those two Marys, they were afraid and happy at the same time. They were afraid because of the mighty works of Heaven…a rock-splitting earthquake…a powerful angel…an empty grave…a dead man come to life. So much happened so fast they could hardly catch their breath! No wonder they were afraid.

But they were happy, too. Happy because a good God was working behind all those wonders. And most of all, happy that their Lord and Best Friend was alive forever after being dead.

Have you ever been afraid and happy at the same time? That's what it's like when God does something great and powerful in your life!

It's the kind of happiness that keeps you wide-eyed with amazement.
It's a kind of fear where you can't help smiling.

It was a lovely Sunday night, but the followers of Jesus weren't out walking in the park. It was a clear, warm evening, but nobody thought about going downtown or meeting friends for a treat or just sitting outside and watching the first shy stars wink through the dome of Heaven.

A group of men and women who loved Jesus were inside a room together with the doors closed and locked. Why do you suppose they locked the doors?

They were *afraid*, that's why!

The same people who had arrested Jesus might want to arrest them, too. The people who had just killed Jesus on the cross might want to kill them, too.

So they had the windows closed and the doors locked tight. They were all crowded into a stuffy room looking at each other, not knowing what to do next.

Sometimes that's the way it is when you are afraid or worried. You don't feel like going anywhere. You don't feel like doing anything. You don't feel like seeing anybody. You don't feel like saying anything. All you want to do is close the doors and lock them; all you want to do is hide.

What if someone had knocked on the door that night? What would Jesus' followers have done? They might have said, "Go away! Nobody's home!" Or someone might have put his finger to his lips and whispered, "Shhhhh! Don't say anything. Maybe he'll go away."

Well, that very night Someone *did* come to visit with them.

Someone came right into the room where everyone was.

But that Someone did not come in through the front door. That Someone did not come in through the back door, the side door, or a window.

Suddenly, that Someone was just *there*.

That Someone was Jesus. Yes, He had been killed! Yes, He had been closed up in a tomb! But now, by the power of God, He was alive again. And there He was—right in the middle of them—looking around the room into the wide eyes of His frightened friends. Do you suppose He was smiling? (Yes, I think so, too.)

*Jesus came and stood right in the middle of them and said, "Peace be with you." After he said this, he showed them his hands and his side. The followers were thrilled when they saw the Lord.* (John 20:19-20)

Do you think those friends of Jesus might have been afraid when He suddenly popped into their hiding place? Think how it would have been. One minute you're looking at a lamp across the room, and

the next instant your eyes are full of Jesus. Yes, they might have been startled. But only for a moment! Then they were so excited and happy to see Jesus that they forgot all about locked doors, shuttered windows, and being afraid.

What an amazing night that was! One minute they were all sitting around in a dim, gloomy room behind bolted doors…and then…faster than the blink of an eye…Jesus was there with them, as close as could be.

I think Jesus must have enjoyed surprising His friends like that, don't you? I think He must have enjoyed taking away the fear from their hearts and giving them joy instead. I think He must have been pleased to show them He could be wherever they were—even when they thought they were hiding.

Do you know what? I think He still likes to do that.

No, I've never seen Him appear in the middle of a room. (I wish He would!) But sometimes

　…when I have felt sad

　…or afraid…or lonely

　…sometimes when I am alone in a room

　…with the doors locked

　…with the curtains closed

He suddenly comes to be very near me.

I don't see Him come. I don't hear Him come. But all the same, I know He is there. And He takes the fear out of my heart and puts joy there instead.

JESUS CAME
AND STOOD
RIGHT IN THE
MIDDLE OF THEM
AND SAID,
"PEACE BE
WITH YOU."
JOHN 20:19

What if I told you…"Yes"? Would you be very surprised?

Would you be surprised to know the Bible tells us we must *fear* the Lord? It's really true. Here is how one man named Elihu explained it his friend Job:

*We cannot look at the sun. It is too bright when the winds have cleared away the clouds. And neither can we gaze at the terrible brightness of God breaking forth from heaven. He is clothed in the brightest of light. We cannot even think of the power of the Almighty. Yet he is so fair and merciful that he does not destroy us. No wonder men everywhere fear him!* (Job 37:21-24, SLB)

Does that mean we don't want to be close to God and love Him and serve Him? No, not at all! The Bible says:

*Be sure to fear the Lord and serve him faithfully with all your heart; consider what great things he has done for you.* (1 Samuel 12:24, NIV)

What does it mean, then, for you and me to *fear* our God?

Imagine with me for a minute or two. Imagine that behind your house you have an observatory. That's the name for a round building—big as a barn—with a very large telescope poking through the roof. But your telescope isn't just "large"…it's *gigantic*. It's the most colossal, powerful telescope the world has ever seen. And it's yours! (A present from a very rich uncle in California.)

While other kids play computer games or watch TV after they finish their dinner and homework at night, you like to grab a couple of your mom's best chocolate chip cookies and head right out to your telescope. Well who wouldn't want to do that? Every astronomer in the world would be jealous of your telescope (and probably of your mom's cookies, too).

Most telescopes have little eye-pieces to look through. But *your* telescope lets you crawl right up inside. Your telescope lets you see and hear and feel things as if you were really right there.

When you aim your telescope at the planets, you don't just see little pea-sized blobs of light as you might through an ordinary telescope. You feel like you're actually standing on those strange, far away worlds.

…As though you were hiking through the knife-sharp mountains of Mercury, feeling the hot, orange gravel crunch under your sneakers.

…As though you were swept off your feet and sucked into a raging, purple storm on Jupiter.

…As though you were fighting to keep your

balance on the glowing, midnight ice fields of cold, lonely Neptune.

And when you point yourself at the *stars*…oh my! You're not looking at cute little twinkly sparkles (like some lady's diamond earrings), you're dropping into the middle of blazing suns, blasting up fountains of white fire that could swallow a hundred earths. You're soaring over the simmering red vastness of dying stars. You're squinting at the throbbing blue-white radiance of new stars searing their way through the blackness of space. You're seeing impossibly distant galaxies and swirling clouds of dust and gas, shot through with flaming rainbows.

It's just plain *scary* looking through that telescope.

Sometimes you have to pull away, go outside, and flop down on the cool grass for a while until your head stops spinning.

How could anything be so vast, so powerful, so bright, so eye-burning beautiful? It gives you goose-bumps. It makes your mouth go dry. It makes your legs weak. Sometimes you find yourself wanting to yell, *"Oh, Wow!"* …but the words come out in a croak.

You're amazed and shaken by what you see. You feel so very small. Your mind feels overwhelmed. *But you still love to look through it every chance you get!* Sometimes, when you speak to others about what you see, you feel like whispering, numb with wonder. At other times you feel like leaping straight up and hollering for pure joy.

That's a little bit what it's like to fear our God.

He is so much brighter and more frightening and awesome than all the wonders of the universe. Why? Because He *created* all those things. The spinning galaxies with their long, stardust arms and trillions of flaming suns are simply the work of His hands. How much greater He is than all that He has made!

It is right and good to feel some fear when we think about God and His power. David tells us:

*Obey the LORD with great fear.*
*Be happy, but tremble.* (Psalm 2:11)

This is a right and good kind of fear. This is a kind of fear that says I respect God and honor God and bow down low before His mighty majesty. He is King of all kings and Lord of all lords. No one can begin to explain His endless power, His shining goodness, or His terrible beauty.

How good is this fear of our great God? The Bible just spills over with promises for those who truly fear His name!

Fearing Him (and loving Him with all our heart at the same time) is the best thing we could ever do. Here is what David said about it—and I get the feeling he was just about to run out of words.

*But from everlasting to everlasting*
*the LORD's love is with those who fear him…*
*You who belong to the LORD, fear him!*
*Those who fear him will have everything*
*they need.* (Psalms 103:17, NIV; 34:9)

You see? The fear of the Lord is all wrapped up with many wonderful promises. What kind of promises? Well, promises that tell us…

how He stores up goodness for us in the treasure cities of Heaven…

how He guides our steps along dark and lonely paths…

how He loves us with a tender Father-love.

People who truly fear the Lord get to find out about the protection of mighty angels, help for their every need, long, good years of living, a sweet fountain of life that bubbles up and never goes dry.

Through our lives we may be afraid of many little things (though they don't seem little to us). And those fears make us sad and worried and they steal our joy. But the fear of the Lord is the greatest of fears—the *king* of fears—that can drive out the smaller fears that weigh us down and darken our days. The fear of the Lord is like a burning sunrise that chases shadows out of a valley.

And the fear of the Lord will never steal our joy. It will bring us more joy than we can begin to hold.

**E**verybody is afraid of something. What makes you afraid may not scare me at all. And what makes me afraid may make you want to laugh right out loud. 🌿 The truth is, I don't know or understand all of your fears, and you don't know or understand all of mine. But God knows about them all...yours and mine...great and small...the ones we can talk and joke about, and the ones we've never told to anyone. 🌿 He loves us so much. And the farther we run into the golden warmth of that forever-love, the more those old fears will melt away like frost in the morning sun.